PERSONAL INFORMATION

Name:

Address:

Telephone: Email:

Employer:

Address:

Telephone: Email:

MEDICAL INFORMATION

Physician: Telephone:

Allergies:

Medications:

Blood Type:

Insurer:

IN CASE OF EMERGENCY, NOTIFY

Name:

Address:

Telephone: Relationship:

ISBN 978-1-68322-614-7; 978-1-944836-42-9

Published by DayMaker, an imprint of Barbour Publishing, Inc., 1810 Barbour Drive, Uhrichsville, Ohio 44683, www.barbourbooks.com

Our mission is to inspire the world with the life-changing message of the Bible.

Member of the
Evangelical Christian
Publishers Association

Printed in China.

TOO BLESSED
to be
STRESSED

Debora M. Coty

2019 PLANNER

DAYMAKER™
An Imprint of Barbour Publishing, Inc.

Introduction

It's easy to get bogged down in the responsibilities, to-do lists, and schedules of everyday life. But God gives us each day to live and thrive in His love—to embrace the grace He freely provides for all of our ups, downs, and in-betweens.

Take time from your busy life to get your heart back to a place of peace. This planner is a good way to start. Use it to assist in the organization of the daily grind, and allow the readings and scripture to bless your soul all 365 days of 2019.

YEAR AT A GLANCE

JANUARY

S	M	T	W	T	F	S
		1	2	3	4	5
6	7	8	9	10	11	12
13	14	15	16	17	18	19
20	21	22	23	24	25	26
27	28	29	30	31		

FEBRUARY

S	M	T	W	T	F	S
					1	2
3	4	5	6	7	8	9
10	11	12	13	14	15	16
17	18	19	20	21	22	23
24	25	26	27	28		

MAY

S	M	T	W	T	F	S
			1	2	3	4
5	6	7	8	9	10	11
12	13	14	15	16	17	18
19	20	21	22	23	24	25
26	27	28	29	30	31	

JUNE

S	M	T	W	T	F	S
						1
2	3	4	5	6	7	8
9	10	11	12	13	14	15
16	17	18	19	20	21	22
23	24	25	26	27	28	29
30						

SEPTEMBER

S	M	T	W	T	F	S
1	2	3	4	5	6	7
8	9	10	11	12	13	14
15	16	17	18	19	20	21
22	23	24	25	26	27	28
29	30					

OCTOBER

S	M	T	W	T	F	S
		1	2	3	4	5
6	7	8	9	10	11	12
13	14	15	16	17	18	19
20	21	22	23	24	25	26
27	28	29	30	31		

2019

MARCH

S	M	T	W	T	F	S
					1	2
3	4	5	6	7	8	9
10	11	12	13	14	15	16
17	18	19	20	21	22	23
24	25	26	27	28	29	30
31						

APRIL

S	M	T	W	T	F	S
	1	2	3	4	5	6
7	8	9	10	11	12	13
14	15	16	17	18	19	20
21	22	23	24	25	26	27
28	29	30				

JULY

S	M	T	W	T	F	S
	1	2	3	4	5	6
7	8	9	10	11	12	13
14	15	16	17	18	19	20
21	22	23	24	25	26	27
28	29	30	31			

AUGUST

S	M	T	W	T	F	S
				1	2	3
4	5	6	7	8	9	10
11	12	13	14	15	16	17
18	19	20	21	22	23	24
25	26	27	28	29	30	31

NOVEMBER

S	M	T	W	T	F	S
					1	2
3	4	5	6	7	8	9
10	11	12	13	14	15	16
17	18	19	20	21	22	23
24	25	26	27	28	29	30

DECEMBER

S	M	T	W	T	F	S
1	2	3	4	5	6	7
8	9	10	11	12	13	14
15	16	17	18	19	20	21
22	23	24	25	26	27	28
29	30	31				

NOVEMBER 2018

SUNDAY	MONDAY	TUESDAY	WEDNESDAY
28	29	30	31
4	5	6 *Election Day*	7
11	12 *Veterans Day*	13	14
18	19	20	21
25	26	27	28

THURSDAY	FRIDAY	SATURDAY
1	2	3
8	9	10
15	16	17
22	23	24
Thanksgiving Day		
29	30	1

OCTOBER

S	M	T	W	T	F	S
		1	2	3	4	5	6
7	8	9	10	11	12	13
14	15	16	17	18	19	20
21	22	23	24	25	26	27
28	29	30	31			

DECEMBER

S	M	T	W	T	F	S
						1
2	3	4	5	6	7	8
9	10	11	12	13	14	15
16	17	18	19	20	21	22
23	24	25	26	27	28	29
30	31					

WHAT ARE YOU TELLING YOURSELF?

Positive self-talk isn't just crucial in sports; it's a huge part of everyday stress management. When we tell ourselves something over and over, we eventually buy into it and it becomes a part of our inner makeup, our self-esteem, our performance motivation—for better or worse. In essence, we choose our attitude and that attitude dictates our stress level.

"Okay, that first soufflé flopped, but so did Julia Child's. I'll make a few adjustments and the next one will be the chef d'oeuvre." When we choose an upbeat attitude, our outlook becomes much more optimistic and consequently less stress producing.

GOALS *for this* MONTH

○ ....
○ ....
○ ....
○ ....
○ ....
○ ....
○ ....
○ ....
○ ....
○ ....
○ ....
○ ....
○ ....
○ ....
○ ....
○ ....
○ ....
○ ....

Carefully guard your thoughts
because they are the source of true life.
PROVERBS 4:23 CEV

NOVEMBER

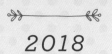

2018

S	M	T	W	T	F	S
				1	2	3
4	5	6	7	8	9	10
11	12	13	14	15	16	17
18	19	20	21	22	23	24
25	26	27	28	29	30	

Dear Papa God, please help me not to ignore
the signs that I'm overdoing it in life. Help me to
put You first, prioritize wisely, and bask in the
peace and rest that will result. Amen.

4—SUNDAY

5—MONDAY

6—TUESDAY   *Election Day*

7—WEDNESDAY

....
....
....
....

8—THURSDAY

....
....
....
....

9—FRIDAY

....
....
....
....

10—SATURDAY

....
....
....
....

*The Master said, "Martha, dear Martha, you're fussing
far too much and getting yourself worked up over nothing.
One thing only is essential, and Mary has chosen it—
it's the main course, and won't be taken from her."*

LUKE 10:41–42 MSG

NOVEMBER

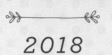

2018

S	M	T	W	T	F	S
				1	2	3
4	5	6	7	8	9	10
11	12	13	14	15	16	17
18	19	20	21	22	23	24
25	26	27	28	29	30	

Dear Papa God, I want to develop a constant
habit of thankfulness. Please surround me
with friends who want this, too. Amen.

11—SUNDAY   *Veterans Day*

....

....

....

....

12—MONDAY

....

....

....

....

13—TUESDAY

....

....

....

....

14—WEDNESDAY

....

....

....

....

15—THURSDAY

....

....

....

....

16—FRIDAY

....

....

....

....

17—SATURDAY

....

....

....

....

*The Lord's kindness never fails! If he had not
been merciful, we would have been destroyed. The Lord
can always be trusted to show mercy each morning.*

LAMENTATIONS 3:22-23 CEV

NOVEMBER

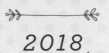

2018

S	M	T	W	T	F	S
				1	2	3
4	5	6	7	8	9	10
11	12	13	14	15	16	17
18	19	20	21	22	23	24
25	26	27	28	29	30	

No matter what we've done, Papa God
can repair, restore, and revitalize the remnants
of our lives for His higher glory.

18—SUNDAY

....

....

....

....

19—MONDAY

....

....

....

....

20—TUESDAY

....

....

....

....

21—WEDNESDAY

....
....
....
....

22—THURSDAY   *Thanksgiving Day*

....
....
....
....

23—FRIDAY

....
....
....
....

24—SATURDAY

....
....
....
....

There is no condemnation for those who belong
to Christ Jesus. And because you belong to Him,
the power of the life-giving Spirit has freed you
from the power of sin that leads to death.

ROMANS 8:1-2 NLT

NOVEMBER–DECEMBER

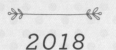

2018

S	M	T	W	T	F	S
				1	2	3
4	5	6	7	8	9	10
11	12	13	14	15	16	17
18	19	20	21	22	23	24
25	26	27	28	29	30	

Dear Papa God, I want to obey You in all things.
When I fail, please keep drawing me back to a right
relationship with You so that I can be filled with
joy and peace, not depression and fear. Amen.

25—SUNDAY

26—MONDAY

27—TUESDAY

28—WEDNESDAY

....

....

....

....

29—THURSDAY

....

....

....

....

30—FRIDAY

....

....

....

....

1—SATURDAY

....

....

....

....

This is love for God: to keep his commands.
And his commands are not burdensome.

1 JOHN 5:3 NIV

DECEMBER 2018

SUNDAY	MONDAY	TUESDAY	WEDNESDAY
25	26	27	28
2 *Hanukkah Begins at Sundown*	3	4	5
9	10	11	12
16	17	18	19
23 30	24 *Christmas Eve* *New Year's Eve* 31	25 *Christmas Day*	26

THURSDAY	FRIDAY	SATURDAY
29	30	1
6	7	8
13	14	15
20	21 *First Day of Winter*	22
27	28	29

NOVEMBER

S	M	T	W	T	F	S
					1	2	3
4	5	6	7	8	9	10
11	12	13	14	15	16	17
18	19	20	21	22	23	24
25	26	27	28	29	30

JANUARY

S	M	T	W	T	F	S
		1	2	3	4	5
6	7	8	9	10	11	12
13	14	15	16	17	18	19
20	21	22	23	24	25	26
27	28	29	30	31

SUPERNATURAL GRACE

We all make mistakes—some knowingly, some not. We inadvertently hurt people at times. We let people down, trample feelings, don't live up to expectations. But it's not just careless or bad behavior at stake. Make no mistake, sister, guilt is a spiritual battle.

Many of us are spiritually schizophrenic like the apostle Paul in Romans 7:15 (MSG): "What I don't understand about myself is that I decide one way, but then I act another, doing things I absolutely despise."

And then guilt sets in like wet cement.

Even when we ask for forgiveness, sometimes our guilt brakes don't engage, and self-persecution just keeps barreling full speed ahead. That's when we have to allow Papa God to override the gears and stall out our revving self-condemnation engine with His supernatural grace.

GOALS *for this* MONTH

- ○ ....
- ○ ....
- ○ ....
- ○ ....
- ○ ....
- ○ ....
- ○ ....
- ○ ....
- ○ ....
- ○ ....
- ○ ....
- ○ ....
- ○ ....
- ○ ....
- ○ ....
- ○ ....
- ○ ....
- ○ ....
- ○ ....

Be strong in the grace that is in Christ Jesus.
2 TIMOTHY 2:1 NIV

DECEMBER

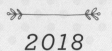

2018

S	M	T	W	T	F	S
						1
2	3	4	5	6	7	8
9	10	11	12	13	14	15
16	17	18	19	20	21	22
23	24	25	26	27	28	29
30	31					

By remembering what Papa God has already
done for us through Christ, we'll develop miracle
memory. He defeated the instigator of fear at
the cross, and He'll do it again. And again.

2—SUNDAY   *Hanukkah Begins at Sundown*

....

....

....

....

3—MONDAY

....

....

....

....

4—TUESDAY

....

....

....

....

5—WEDNESDAY

....

....

....

....

6—THURSDAY

....

....

....

....

7—FRIDAY

....

....

....

....

8—SATURDAY

....

....

....

....

*For his unfailing love toward those who fear him is as great
as the height of the heavens above the earth. He has removed
our sins as far from us as the east is from the west.*

PSALM 103:11-12 NLT

DECEMBER

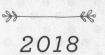

2018

S	M	T	W	T	F	S
						1
2	3	4	5	6	7	8
9	10	11	12	13	14	15
16	17	18	19	20	21	22
23	24	25	26	27	28	29
30	31					

The way we really become beautiful is
by doing something beautiful for God.

9—SUNDAY

....

....

....

....

10—MONDAY

....

....

....

....

11—TUESDAY

....

....

....

....

12—WEDNESDAY

13—THURSDAY

14—FRIDAY

15—SATURDAY

The righteous person may have many troubles,
but the LORD delivers him from them all.

PSALM 34:19 NIV

DECEMBER

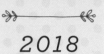

2018

S	M	T	W	T	F	S
						1
2	3	4	5	6	7	8
9	10	11	12	13	14	15
16	17	18	19	20	21	22
23	24	25	26	27	28	29
30	31					

If I'm serious about emulating Christ, there shouldn't
be a difference between my inward and outward image.
My Christian persona should be the real deal, not just for show.

16—SUNDAY

17—MONDAY

18—TUESDAY

19—WEDNESDAY

....
....
....
....

20—THURSDAY

....
....
....
....

21—FRIDAY   *First Day of Winter*

....
....
....
....

22—SATURDAY

....
....
....
....

*Women who claim to be devoted to God should make
themselves attractive by the good things they do.*

1 TIMOTHY 2:10 NLT

DECEMBER

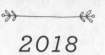

2018

S	M	T	W	T	F	S
						1
2	3	4	5	6	7	8
9	10	11	12	13	14	15
16	17	18	19	20	21	22
23	24	25	26	27	28	29
30	31					

Dear Papa God, please help me to get creative in finding quiet times to connect with You. Amen.

23—SUNDAY

24—MONDAY   *Christmas Eve*

25—TUESDAY   *Christmas Day*

26—WEDNESDAY

27—THURSDAY

28—FRIDAY

29—SATURDAY

*But Jesus would often go to some place
where he could be alone and pray.*

LUKE 5:16 CEV

JANUARY 2019

SUNDAY	MONDAY	TUESDAY	WEDNESDAY
30	31	1 *New Year's Day*	2
6	7	8	9
13	14	15	16
20	21 *Martin Luther King Jr. Day*	22	23
27	28	29	30

THURSDAY	FRIDAY	SATURDAY
3	4	5
10	11	12
17	18	19
24	25	26
31	1	2

DECEMBER

S	M	T	W	T	F	S
						1
2	3	4	5	6	7	8
9	10	11	12	13	14	15
16	17	18	19	20	21	22
23	24	25	26	27	28	29
30	31					

FEBRUARY

S	M	T	W	T	F	S
					1	2
3	4	5	6	7	8	9
10	11	12	13	14	15	16
17	18	19	20	21	22	23
24	25	26	27	28		

FEAR CAN BE A GOOD THING

Papa God gave us the emotion of fear for good reason. It serves a useful purpose—to motivate us, move us forward, and keep us from making mistakes. Sometimes fear saves us from ourselves. Why else would we faithfully squash our bosom buddies flat with mammograms without the possibility of that frightening *C* word invading our bodies? We could be out pounding the pavement if fear of losing our jobs didn't motivate us to get our reports in on time.

It's when fear becomes controlling that it debilitates. When it alters our course from the splendid women Papa God intended us to be and makes us settle for a wimpy, whiny imitation. Or when it begins to dictate our thoughts and behavior.

GOALS *for this* MONTH

○ ....
○ ....
○ ....
○ ....
○ ....
○ ....
○ ....
○ ....
○ ....
○ ....
○ ....
○ ....
○ ....
○ ....
○ ....
○ ....
○ ....

*"Don't panic. I'm with you. There's no need to fear
for I'm your God. I'll give you strength. I'll help you.
I'll hold you steady, keep a firm grip on you."*

ISAIAH 41:10 MSG

DECEMBER 2018– JANUARY

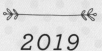

2019

S	M	T	W	T	F	S
						1	2	3	4	5

S	M	T	W	T	F	S
					1	2	3	4	5
6	7	8	9	10	11	12
13	14	15	16	17	18	19
20	21	22	23	24	25	26
27	28	29	30	31		

Dear Papa God, thank You for fully understanding our learning process of trust. I'm so grateful for Your amazing patience and love for me. Amen.

30—SUNDAY

....
....
....
....

31—MONDAY *New Year's Eve*

....
....
....
....

1—TUESDAY *New Year's Day*

....
....
....
....

2—WEDNESDAY

....

....

....

....

3—THURSDAY

....

....

....

....

4—FRIDAY

....

....

....

....

5—SATURDAY

....

....

....

....

Those who know your name trust in you, for you,
LORD, have never forsaken those who seek you.

PSALM 9:10 NIV

JANUARY

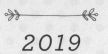

2019

S	M	T	W	T	F	S
		1	2	3	4	5
6	7	8	9	10	11	12
13	14	15	16	17	18	19
20	21	22	23	24	25	26
27	28	29	30	31		

Author Adel Bestavros said, "Patience with others is love; patience with self is hope; patience with God is faith." Think on that.

6—SUNDAY

....

....

....

....

7—MONDAY

....

....

....

....

8—TUESDAY

....

....

....

....

9—WEDNESDAY

....

....

....

....

10—THURSDAY

....

....

....

....

11—FRIDAY

....

....

....

....

12—SATURDAY

....

....

....

....

Learn to be patient, so that you will please
God and be given what he has promised.

HEBREWS 10:36 CEV

JANUARY

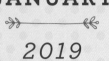

2019

S	M	T	W	T	F	S
		1	2	3	4	5
6	7	8	9	10	11	12
13	14	15	16	17	18	19
20	21	22	23	24	25	26
27	28	29	30	31		

Dear Papa God, I want the power, love,
and self-discipline to live a truly free life that is
filled with Your light and brings You glory. Amen.

13—SUNDAY

....

....

....

....

14—MONDAY

....

....

....

....

15—TUESDAY

....

....

....

....

16—WEDNESDAY

17—THURSDAY

18—FRIDAY

19—SATURDAY

*"If the Son makes you free,
you will be free indeed."*
JOHN 8:36 NASB

JANUARY

2019

S	M	T	W	T	F	S
		1	2	3	4	5
6	7	8	9	10	11	12
13	14	15	16	17	18	19
20	21	22	23	24	25	26
27	28	29	30	31		

Forgiveness isn't really optional for believers—
in order for us to receive forgiveness, we must give it.

20—SUNDAY

21—MONDAY   *Martin Luther King Jr. Day*

22—TUESDAY

23—WEDNESDAY

....

....

....

....

24—THURSDAY

....

....

....

....

25—FRIDAY

....

....

....

....

26—SATURDAY

....

....

....

....

*If you forgive others for the wrongs they do to you,
your Father in heaven will forgive you. But if you don't
forgive others, your Father will not forgive your sins.*
Matthew 6:14-15 CEV

JANUARY– FEBRUARY

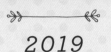

2019

S	M	T	W	T	F	S
		1	2	3	4	5
6	7	8	9	10	11	12
13	14	15	16	17	18	19
20	21	22	23	24	25	26
27	28	29	30	31		

Dear Papa God, may I never be too prideful to do anything You ask me to do. Help me to serve others and do all things for Your glory. Amen.

27—SUNDAY

....
....
....
....

28—MONDAY

....
....
....
....

29—TUESDAY

....
....
....
....

30—WEDNESDAY

....

....

....

....

31—THURSDAY

....

....

....

....

1—FRIDAY

....

....

....

....

2—SATURDAY

....

....

....

....

Show love in everything you do.
1 CORINTHIANS 16:14 CEV

FEBRUARY 2019

SUNDAY	MONDAY	TUESDAY	WEDNESDAY
27	28	29	30
3	4	5	6
10	11	12	13
17	18	19	20
	Presidents' Day		
24	25	26	27

THURSDAY	FRIDAY	SATURDAY
31	1	2
7	8	9
14 *Valentine's Day*	15	16
21	22	23
28	1	2

JANUARY

S	M	T	W	T	F	S
			1	2	3	4	5
6	7	8	9	10	11	12
13	14	15	16	17	18	19
20	21	22	23	24	25	26
27	28	29	30	31		

MARCH

S	M	T	W	T	F	S
					1	2
3	4	5	6	7	8	9
10	11	12	13	14	15	16
17	18	19	20	21	22	23
24	25	26	27	28	29	30
31						

WHAT ARE YOU LOOKING FOR?

We all struggle to keep our eyes on the Creator and not on the created (ourselves). I actually cringed when a man in my couples Bible study commented, "My, Debbie, you look very wholesome tonight."

Wholesome? That was not the look I was going for. Attractive, lovely, feminine, ravishing—even color coordinated would have been welcomed. But wholesome? Isn't cracked wheat wholesome?

Then the more I thought about it, I realized that was actually one of the nicest compliments I've ever received. Wholesome is precisely the way Papa God desires for me to be perceived, especially by men who aren't my husband.

GOALS *for this* MONTH

- ○ ....
- ○ ....
- ○ ....
- ○ ....
- ○ ....
- ○ ....
- ○ ....
- ○ ....
- ○ ....
- ○ ....
- ○ ....
- ○ ....
- ○ ....
- ○ ....
- ○ ....
- ○ ....
- ○ ....
- ○ ....

God doesn't require attention-getting devices.

MATTHEW 6:18 MSG

FEBRUARY

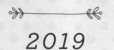

2019

S	M	T	W	T	F	S
					1	2
3	4	5	6	7	8	9
10	11	12	13	14	15	16
17	18	19	20	21	22	23
24	25	26	27	28		

Dear Papa God, You are so good to me, and I don't thank You enough. Help me to see and count my blessings daily for a lifestyle of gratitude. Amen.

3—SUNDAY

....

....

....

....

4—MONDAY

....

....

....

....

5—TUESDAY

....

....

....

....

6—WEDNESDAY

....

....

....

....

7—THURSDAY

....

....

....

....

8—FRIDAY

....

....

....

....

9—SATURDAY

....

....

....

....

*"But as for me and my household,
we will serve the LORD."*

JOSHUA 24:15 NIV

FEBRUARY

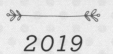

2019

S	M	T	W	T	F	S
					1	2
3	4	5	6	7	8	9
10	11	12	13	14	15	16
17	18	19	20	21	22	23
24	25	26	27	28		

Dear Papa God, please arm me with Your Word.
Help me to be ready for any spiritual battle. Amen.

10—SUNDAY

11—MONDAY

12—TUESDAY

13—WEDNESDAY

....
....
....
....

14—THURSDAY

Valentine's Day

....
....
....
....

15—FRIDAY

....
....
....
....

16—SATURDAY

....
....
....
....

For the word of God is alive and powerful.
It is sharper than the sharpest two-edged sword.
HEBREWS 4:12 NLT

FEBRUARY

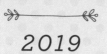

2019

S	M	T	W	T	F	S
					1	2
3	4	5	6	7	8	9
10	11	12	13	14	15	16
17	18	19	20	21	22	23
24	25	26	27	28		

Dear Papa God, please help me to keep my
eyes lifted up to You, not focusing on my troubles,
but focusing on Your power to come to my rescue. Amen.

17—SUNDAY

....
....
....
....

18—MONDAY   *Presidents' Day*

....
....
....
....

19—TUESDAY

....
....
....
....

20—WEDNESDAY

21—THURSDAY

22—FRIDAY

23—SATURDAY

*I lift up my eyes to the mountains—where
does my help come from? My help comes
from the LORD, the Maker of heaven and earth.*

PSALM 121:1-2 NIV

FEBRUARY–
MARCH

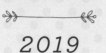

2019

S	M	T	W	T	F	S
					1	2
3	4	5	6	7	8	9
10	11	12	13	14	15	16
17	18	19	20	21	22	23
24	25	26	27	28		

Eligibility for entrance into heaven isn't graded on a curve; we don't get there by being better than someone else. We get there by faith alone. . .in Christ alone. . .by grace alone.

24—SUNDAY

25—MONDAY

26—TUESDAY

27—WEDNESDAY

....

....

....

....

28—THURSDAY

....

....

....

....

1—FRIDAY

....

....

....

....

2—SATURDAY

....

....

....

....

For by grace you have been saved through faith;
and that not of yourselves, it is the gift of God;
not as a result of works, so that no one may boast.

EPHESIANS 2:8-9 NASB

MARCH 2019

SUNDAY	MONDAY	TUESDAY	WEDNESDAY
24	25	26	27
3	4	5	6 *Ash Wednesday*
10	11	12	13
17 *St. Patrick's Day*	18	19	20 *First Day of Spring*
24 31	25	26	27

THURSDAY	FRIDAY	SATURDAY
28	1	2
7	8	9
14	15	16
21	22	23
28	29	30

FEBRUARY

S	M	T	W	T	F	S
					1	2
3	4	5	6	7	8	9
10	11	12	13	14	15	16
17	18	19	20	21	22	23
24	25	26	27	28		

APRIL

S	M	T	W	T	F	S
	1	2	3	4	5	6
7	8	9	10	11	12	13
14	15	16	17	18	19	20
21	22	23	24	25	26	27
28	29	30				

BUILD OTHERS UP

The apostle Paul correlates wholesomeness with the "edification" of others in Ephesians 4:29 (NASB). The definition of *edification* is "improvement in morality." So what Paul is saying is that we should present ourselves to others in a way that improves them—builds up their character—not only by our appearance, but in our speech and actions as well.

That means no pretenses, false fronts, or role-playing to build ourselves up in the eyes of others. Why? Because our focus is on them, not us.

Wow—what a relief! How much easier to be one person. . .inside and out. . .to any audience. . .at all times.

GOALS *for this* MONTH

- ○
- ○
- ○
- ○
- ○
- ○
- ○
- ○
- ○
- ○
- ○
- ○
- ○
- ○
- ○
- ○
- ○

Let no unwholesome word proceed from your mouth, but only such a word as is good for edification according to the need of the moment, so that it will give grace to those who hear.

EPHESIANS 4:29 NASB

MARCH

2019

S	M	T	W	T	F	S
					1	2
3	4	5	6	7	8	9
10	11	12	13	14	15	16
17	18	19	20	21	22	23
24	25	26	27	28	29	30
31						

Dear Papa God, I crave an extended retreat
with You to renew and refresh our relationship.
Please help me to make the time. Amen.

3—SUNDAY

....
....
....
....

4—MONDAY

....
....
....
....

5—TUESDAY

....
....
....
....

6—WEDNESDAY

Ash Wednesday

7—THURSDAY

8—FRIDAY

9—SATURDAY

"Come unto me, all you who are weary and burdened, and I will give you rest. Take my yoke upon you and learn from me, for I am gentle and humble in heart, and you will find rest for your souls. For my yoke is easy and my burden is light."

MATTHEW 11:28-30 NIV

MARCH

2019

S	M	T	W	T	F	S
					1	2
3	4	5	6	7	8	9
10	11	12	13	14	15	16
17	18	19	20	21	22	23
24	25	26	27	28	29	30
31						

Dear Papa God, help me to realize it doesn't take much, even just a quick phone call, to let someone know how much I care. Help me to be a good friend and encourager. Amen.

10—SUNDAY

....

....

....

....

11—MONDAY

....

....

....

....

12—TUESDAY

....

....

....

....

13—WEDNESDAY

14—THURSDAY

15—FRIDAY

16—SATURDAY

*We should keep on encouraging each other
to be thoughtful and to do helpful things.*
HEBREWS 10:24 CEV

MARCH

2019

S	M	T	W	T	F	S
					1	2
3	4	5	6	7	8	9
10	11	12	13	14	15	16
17	18	19	20	21	22	23
24	25	26	27	28	29	30
31						

Dear Papa God, Your Word truly is a
lamp to my feet and a light to my path.
It is such a blessing to follow You. Amen.

17—SUNDAY   *St. Patrick's Day*

....

....

....

....

18—MONDAY

....

....

....

....

19—TUESDAY

....

....

....

....

20—WEDNESDAY

First Day of Spring

....

....

....

....

21—THURSDAY

....

....

....

....

22—FRIDAY

....

....

....

....

23—SATURDAY

....

....

....

....

*Your word is a lamp to guide my
feet and a light for my path.*
PSALM 119:105 NLT

MARCH

❧⟶⟵❧

2019

S	M	T	W	T	F	S
					1	2
3	4	5	6	7	8	9
10	11	12	13	14	15	16
17	18	19	20	21	22	23
24	25	26	27	28	29	30
31						

One of God's very best gifts is our children.

24—SUNDAY

....
....
....
....

25—MONDAY

....
....
....
....

26—TUESDAY

....
....
....

27—WEDNESDAY

....

....

....

....

28—THURSDAY

....

....

....

....

29—FRIDAY

....

....

....

....

30—SATURDAY

....

....

....

....

Children are a gift from the Lord;
they are a reward from him.

PSALM 127:3 NLT

APRIL 2019

SUNDAY	MONDAY	TUESDAY	WEDNESDAY
31	1	2	3
7	8	9	10
14	15	16	17
Palm Sunday			
21	22	23	24
Easter Sunday			
28	29	30	1

THURSDAY	FRIDAY	SATURDAY
4	5	6
11	12	13
18	19 *Good Friday/Passover Begins at Sundown*	20
25	26	27
2	3	4

MARCH

S	M	T	W	T	F	S
					1	2
3	4	5	6	7	8	9
10	11	12	13	14	15	16
17	18	19	20	21	22	23
24	25	26	27	28	29	30
31						

MAY

S	M	T	W	T	F	S
			1	2	3	4
5	6	7	8	9	10	11
12	13	14	15	16	17	18
19	20	21	22	23	24	25
26	27	28	29	30	31	

LIFE'S SINKHOLES

There are times in all of our lives when we feel as though we've been swallowed by a sinkhole. Something shakes our world, and the ground beneath our feet falls away. Our sense of normalcy is disrupted and our foundation of security splits wide open, leaving us staring up from the bottom of a deep pit at the life we once knew.

We need to have a dependency on something—or Someone—larger and more powerful than ourselves to lift us out. In fact, the more independent we become, the more likely we are to stubbornly keep wallowing in our sinkholes.

GOALS *for this* MONTH

- ○ ....
- ○ ....
- ○ ....
- ○ ....
- ○ ....
- ○ ....
- ○ ....
- ○ ....
- ○ ....
- ○ ....
- ○ ....
- ○ ....
- ○ ....
- ○ ....
- ○ ....
- ○ ....
- ○ ....
- ○ ....

*The one who is in you is greater
than the one who is in the world.*
1 JOHN 4:4 NIV

MARCH–
APRIL

2019

S	M	T	W	T	F	S
	1	2	3	4	5	6
7	8	9	10	11	12	13
14	15	16	17	18	19	20
21	22	23	24	25	26	27
28	29	30				

Our Father's love itself is what makes us whole and holy;
not anything we can contrive, create, or earn.

31—SUNDAY

....

....

....

....

1—MONDAY

....

....

....

....

2—TUESDAY

....

....

....

....

3—WEDNESDAY

4—THURSDAY

5—FRIDAY

6—SATURDAY

But I trust in you, LORD; I say, "You are my God."
My times are in your hands; deliver me from the
hands of my enemies, from those who pursue me.

PSALM 31:14-15 NIV

APRIL

2019

S	M	T	W	T	F	S
	1	2	3	4	5	6
7	8	9	10	11	12	13
14	15	16	17	18	19	20
21	22	23	24	25	26	27
28	29	30				

Dear Papa God, Your Word absolutely is a light and guide
for my path in life and a healing spring of water when
I'm dry and wounded by this world. Thank You! Amen.

7—SUNDAY

....
....
....
....

8—MONDAY

....
....
....
....

9—TUESDAY

....
....
....
....

10—WEDNESDAY

11—THURSDAY

12—FRIDAY

13—SATURDAY

You are my God. I worship you. In my heart, I long for you,
as I would long for a stream in a scorching desert.

PSALM 63:1 CEV

APRIL

2019

S	M	T	W	T	F	S
		1	2	3	4	5	6
7	8	9	10	11	12	13
14	15	16	17	18	19	20
21	22	23	24	25	26	27
28	29	30				

Trust in our heavenly Father is meant
to literally become a part of us. A lifestyle.

14—SUNDAY   *Palm Sunday*

....

....

....

....

15—MONDAY

....

....

....

....

16—TUESDAY

....

....

....

....

17—WEDNESDAY

....

....

....

....

18—THURSDAY

....

....

....

....

19—FRIDAY   *Good Friday/Passover Begins at Sundown*

....

....

....

....

20—SATURDAY

....

....

....

....

---

*Trust in the LORD with all your heart and lean
not on your own understanding; in all your ways
submit to him, and he will make your paths straight.*

PROVERBS 3:5-6 NIV

APRIL

2019

S	M	T	W	T	F	S
	1	2	3	4	5	6
7	8	9	10	11	12	13
14	15	16	17	18	19	20
21	22	23	24	25	26	27
28	29	30				

Dear Papa God, You are so worthy of my
worship, the only One who is! I want to praise
You wherever I am and in everything I do! Amen.

21—SUNDAY   *Easter Sunday*

....
....
....
....

22—MONDAY

....
....
....
....

23—TUESDAY

....
....
....
....

24—WEDNESDAY

....

....

....

....

25—THURSDAY

....

....

....

....

26—FRIDAY

....

....

....

....

27—SATURDAY

....

....

....

....

"Yet a time is coming and has now come when the true worshipers will worship the Father in the Spirit and in truth, for they are the kind of worshipers the Father seeks."

JOHN 4:23 NIV

MAY 2019

SUNDAY	MONDAY	TUESDAY	WEDNESDAY
28	29	30	1
5	6	7	8
12	13	14	15
Mother's Day			
19	20	21	22
26	27	28	29
	Memorial Day		

THURSDAY	FRIDAY	SATURDAY
2 *National Day of Prayer*	3	4
9	10	11
16	17	18
23	24	25
30	31	1

APRIL

S	M	T	W	T	F	S
		1	2	3	4	5	6
7	8	9	10	11	12	13
14	15	16	17	18	19	20
21	22	23	24	25	26	27
28	29	30				

JUNE

S	M	T	W	T	F	S
						1
2	3	4	5	6	7	8
9	10	11	12	13	14	15
16	17	18	19	20	21	22
23	24	25	26	27	28	29
30						

BE STILL

Many times I'm too busy to allow my heavenly Father to snuggle with me. His arms are open wide, but I fill up my day with checking emails, shopping, working, cleaning, cooking—all the while running over for a token high five or peck on the cheek via a microwave prayer before leaving Him standing there as I return alone to life as I know it.

And then eventually, operating on my own strength, I run out of gas. Maybe Papa God actually wants me to finally run out of energy so that I'll sink into His lap and not fight the rejuvenation He longs to give me. What kind of crazy woman would actually resist resting in the arms of the One who loves her more than life itself?

GOALS *for this* MONTH

○ ....
○ ....
○ ....
○ ....
○ ....
○ ....
○ ....
○ ....
○ ....
○ ....
○ ....
○ ....
○ ....
○ ....
○ ....
○ ....
○ ....
○ ....

"Be still, and know that I am God."

PSALM 46:10 NIV

APRIL–MAY

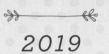

2019

S	M	T	W	T	F	S
				1	2	3	4
5	6	7	8	9	10	11
12	13	14	15	16	17	18
19	20	21	22	23	24	25
26	27	28	29	30	31	

Dear Papa God, my siblings are a blessing, even when we don't see eye to eye. Thank You for them and help me to love and encourage them. Amen.

28—SUNDAY

....

....

....

....

29—MONDAY

....

....

....

....

30—TUESDAY

....

....

....

....

1—WEDNESDAY

2—THURSDAY   *National Day of Prayer*

3—FRIDAY

4—SATURDAY

Be kind and merciful, and forgive others,
just as God forgave you because of Christ.
EPHESIANS 4:32 CEV

MAY

2019

S	M	T	W	T	F	S
			1	2	3	4
5	6	7	8	9	10	11
12	13	14	15	16	17	18
19	20	21	22	23	24	25
26	27	28	29	30	31	

Dear Papa God, please let the story of Ruth encourage me to trust in You more. You are sovereign, and Your plans and timing are perfect. Thank You! Amen.

5—SUNDAY

....

....

....

....

6—MONDAY

....

....

....

....

7—TUESDAY

....

....

....

....

8—WEDNESDAY

....
....
....
....

9—THURSDAY

....
....
....
....

10—FRIDAY

....
....
....
....

11—SATURDAY

....
....
....
....

*Naomi said, "Where did you work today? Whose field was it?
God bless the man who treated you so well!" Then Ruth told
her that she had worked in the field of a man named Boaz.*

RUTH 2:19 CEV

MAY

2019

S	M	T	W	T	F	S
			1	2	3	4
5	6	7	8	9	10	11
12	13	14	15	16	17	18
19	20	21	22	23	24	25
26	27	28	29	30	31	

All the time we spend looking in the mirror,
primping, adjusting, and reinventing ourselves will
be for naught if we're not beautiful from the inside out.

12—SUNDAY   *Mother's Day*

....

....

....

....

13—MONDAY

....

....

....

....

14—TUESDAY

....

....

....

....

15—WEDNESDAY

....

....

....

....

16—THURSDAY

....

....

....

....

17—FRIDAY

....

....

....

....

18—SATURDAY

....

....

....

....

Let the king be enthralled by your beauty;
honor him, for he is your lord.

PSALM 45:11 NIV

MAY

2019

S	M	T	W	T	F	S
			1	2	3	4
5	6	7	8	9	10	11
12	13	14	15	16	17	18
19	20	21	22	23	24	25
26	27	28	29	30	31	

Dear Papa God, when times are hard, please
help me to be deliberate and intentional
about staying faithful to You. Amen.

19—SUNDAY

....
....
....
....

20—MONDAY

....
....
....
....

21—TUESDAY

....
....
....
....

22—WEDNESDAY

23—THURSDAY

24—FRIDAY

25—SATURDAY

Love the LORD, all his people! The LORD preserves those who are true to him, but the proud he pays back in full. Be strong and take heart, all you who hope in the LORD.

PSALM 31:23-24 NIV

MAY–JUNE

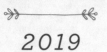

2019

S	M	T	W	T	F	S
			1	2	3	4
5	6	7	8	9	10	11
12	13	14	15	16	17	18
19	20	21	22	23	24	25
26	27	28	29	30	31	

Girlfriends. What would we do without 'em? They are the rare finds who hear the songs down deep in our souls and care enough to sing a duet when we can't manage a solo.

26—SUNDAY

....

....

....

....

27—MONDAY   *Memorial Day*

....

....

....

28—TUESDAY

....

....

....

....

29—WEDNESDAY

....

....

....

....

30—THURSDAY

....

....

....

....

31—FRIDAY

....

....

....

....

1—SATURDAY

....

....

....

....

You are better off to have a friend than to be all alone, because then you will get more enjoyment out of what you earn. If you fall, your friend can help you up. But if you fall without having a friend nearby, you are really in trouble.

ECCLESIASTES 4:9-10 CEV

JUNE 2019

SUNDAY	MONDAY	TUESDAY	WEDNESDAY
26	27	28	29
2	3	4	5
9	10	11	12
16 *Father's Day*	17	18	19
23 / 30	24	25	26

THURSDAY	FRIDAY	SATURDAY
30	31	1
6	7	8
13	14 *Flag Day*	15
20	21 *First Day of Summer*	22
27	28	29

MAY

S	M	T	W	T	F	S
				1	2	3	4
5	6	7	8	9	10	11
12	13	14	15	16	17	18
19	20	21	22	23	24	25
26	27	28	29	30	31	

JULY

S	M	T	W	T	F	S
	1	2	3	4	5	6
7	8	9	10	11	12	13
14	15	16	17	18	19	20
21	22	23	24	25	26	27
28	29	30	31			

CALM IN OUR HEARTS

Jesus doesn't always quell the storms of our lives, does He? Sometimes we have to experience the strength of the wind and waves before we can appreciate the peace He brings. And it might not be external peace at all; our outward circumstances might continue to surge all around us, but that doesn't mean He can't bring us internal peace in the midst of the chaos. "The LORD gives strength to his people; the LORD blesses his people with peace" (Psalm 29:11 NIV).

Sometimes Jesus calms the storm, and sometimes He calms our hearts.

GOALS *for this* MONTH

- ○ ....
- ○ ....
- ○ ....
- ○ ....
- ○ ....
- ○ ....
- ○ ....
- ○ ....
- ○ ....
- ○ ....
- ○ ....
- ○ ....
- ○ ....
- ○ ....
- ○ ....
- ○ ....
- ○ ....
- ○ ....
- ○ ....

May the Lord of peace himself give you peace at all times and in every way. The Lord be with all of you.
2 THESSALONIANS 3:16 NIV

JUNE

2019

Dear Papa God, I need such help with self-control, whether it's in regard to avoiding junk food or taming my tongue or watching my attitude, just to name a few examples. The temptation to give in to my sin nature is great, but Your Spirit is always greater. Amen.

2—SUNDAY

3—MONDAY

4—TUESDAY

5—WEDNESDAY

....

....

....

....

6—THURSDAY

....

....

....

....

7—FRIDAY

....

....

....

....

8—SATURDAY

....

....

....

....

Like a city whose walls are broken through
is a person who lacks self-control.
PROVERBS 25:28 NIV

JUNE

2019

S	M	T	W	T	F	S
						1
2	3	4	5	6	7	8
9	10	11	12	13	14	15
16	17	18	19	20	21	22
23	24	25	26	27	28	29
30						

Faithfulness is the Spirit's star fruit—
symbolizing a glittering star
for our crown in heaven.

9—SUNDAY

10—MONDAY

11—TUESDAY

12—WEDNESDAY

....

....

....

....

13—THURSDAY

....

....

....

....

14—FRIDAY   *Flag Day*

....

....

....

....

15—SATURDAY

....

....

....

....

For we live by faith, not by sight.
2 CORINTHIANS 5:7 NIV

JUNE

2019

S	M	T	W	T	F	S
						1
2	3	4	5	6	7	8
9	10	11	12	13	14	15
16	17	18	19	20	21	22
23	24	25	26	27	28	29
30						

Dear Papa God, at times I feel like being harsh and blunt and loud, and it's hard to stay calm and tender. Please help me to develop more gentleness in my actions and reactions. Amen.

16—SUNDAY   *Father's Day*

....
....
....
....

17—MONDAY

....
....
....
....

18—TUESDAY

....
....
....
....

19—WEDNESDAY

20—THURSDAY

21—FRIDAY   *First Day of Summer*

22—SATURDAY

But you, man of God, flee from all this,
and pursue righteousness, godliness,
faith, love, endurance and gentleness.

1 TIMOTHY 6:11 NIV

JUNE

2019

S	M	T	W	T	F	S
						1
2	3	4	5	6	7	8
9	10	11	12	13	14	15
16	17	18	19	20	21	22
23	24	25	26	27	28	29
30						

Goodness is nothing from within ourselves
but everything from God's orchestration.

23—SUNDAY

....

....

....

....

24—MONDAY

....

....

....

....

25—TUESDAY

....

....

....

....

26—WEDNESDAY

....

....

....

....

27—THURSDAY

....

....

....

....

28—FRIDAY

....

....

....

....

29—SATURDAY

....

....

....

....

Taste and see that the LORD is good;
blessed is the one who takes refuge in him.

PSALM 34:8 NIV

JULY 2019

SUNDAY	MONDAY	TUESDAY	WEDNESDAY
30	1	2	3
7	8	9	10
14	15	16	17
21	22	23	24
28	29	30	31

THURSDAY	FRIDAY	SATURDAY
4	5	6
Independence Day		
11	12	13
18	19	20
25	26	27
1	2	3

JUNE

S	M	T	W	T	F	S
						1
2	3	4	5	6	7	8
9	10	11	12	13	14	15
16	17	18	19	20	21	22
23	24	25	26	27	28	29
30						

AUGUST

S	M	T	W	T	F	S
				1	2	3
4	5	6	7	8	9	10
11	12	13	14	15	16	17
18	19	20	21	22	23	24
25	26	27	28	29	30	31

GET BACK UP

Remember when your little tyke discovered the fine art of equilibrium while learning to ride his bicycle? Concentration, lots of falls, and constant readjustment were necessary for him to finally find the right combination of factors that enabled him to remain upright and in control while careening down the driveway.

Balancing work, faith, and family takes the same kind of determination and focus. Sure, you'll make some mistakes, but after a fall you must pick yourself up, wipe the gravel off your skinned knees, and keep pedaling until you can remain upright and in control.

GOALS *for this* MONTH

- ○ ....
- ○ ....
- ○ ....
- ○ ....
- ○ ....
- ○ ....
- ○ ....
- ○ ....
- ○ ....
- ○ ....
- ○ ....
- ○ ....
- ○ ....
- ○ ....
- ○ ....
- ○ ....
- ○ ....
- ○ ....

We can make our plans, but the
Lord determines our steps.
PROVERBS 16:9 NLT

JUNE–JULY

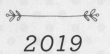

2019

S	M	T	W	T	F	S
		1	2	3	4	5	6
7	8	9	10	11	12	13
14	15	16	17	18	19	20
21	22	23	24	25	26	27
28	29	30	31			

Dear Papa God, I need balance in my schedule.
Please help me to prioritize my time and
tasks in a way that honors You. Amen.

30—SUNDAY

1—MONDAY

2—TUESDAY

3—WEDNESDAY

....

....

....

....

4—THURSDAY   *Independence Day*

....

....

....

....

5—FRIDAY

....

....

....

....

6—SATURDAY

....

....

....

....

*Let God transform you into a new person by changing
the way you think. Then you will learn to know God's
will for you, which is good and pleasing and perfect.*

ROMANS 12:2 NLT

JULY

2019

S	M	T	W	T	F	S
	1	2	3	4	5	6
7	8	9	10	11	12	13
14	15	16	17	18	19	20
21	22	23	24	25	26	27
28	29	30	31			

Dear Papa God, please help me to have
confidence in and seek help constantly from Your
all-powerful Spirit that You've given me. Amen.

7—SUNDAY

....
....
....
....

8—MONDAY

....
....
....
....

9—TUESDAY

....
....
....
....

10—WEDNESDAY

....

....

....

....

11—THURSDAY

....

....

....

....

12—FRIDAY

....

....

....

....

13—SATURDAY

....

....

....

....

*The Spirit of God, who raised Jesus from the dead,
lives in you. And just as God raised Christ Jesus
from the dead, he will give life to your mortal
bodies by this same Spirit living within you.*

ROMANS 8:11 NLT

JULY

2019

S	M	T	W	T	F	S
	1	2	3	4	5	6
7	8	9	10	11	12	13
14	15	16	17	18	19	20
21	22	23	24	25	26	27
28	29	30	31			

God desires only to colorize our black-and-white world and refill it with light and beauty. "Keep company with me and you'll learn to live freely and lightly" (Matthew 11:30 MSG).

14—SUNDAY

....

....

....

....

15—MONDAY

....

....

....

....

16—TUESDAY

....

....

....

....

17—WEDNESDAY

18—THURSDAY

19—FRIDAY

20—SATURDAY

*"Are you tired? Worn out? Burned out on religion?
Come to me. Get away with me and you'll recover
your life. I'll show you how to take a real rest."*

MATTHEW 11:28 MSG

JULY

2019

S	M	T	W	T	F	S
	1	2	3	4	5	6
7	8	9	10	11	12	13
14	15	16	17	18	19	20
21	22	23	24	25	26	27
28	29	30	31			

Dear Papa God, I need to deal with this anger I have, and I need Your help. Please let me give it to You—again and again if need be—and thank You for taking it. Amen.

21—SUNDAY

22—MONDAY

23—TUESDAY

24—WEDNESDAY

....

....

....

....

25—THURSDAY

....

....

....

....

26—FRIDAY

....

....

....

....

27—SATURDAY

....

....

....

....

*Go ahead and be angry. You do well to be angry—but don't
use your anger as fuel for revenge. And don't stay angry. . . .
Don't give the devil that kind of foothold in your life.*

EPHESIANS 4:26–27 MSG

JULY–AUGUST

2019

S	M	T	W	T	F	S
	1	2	3	4	5	6
7	8	9	10	11	12	13
14	15	16	17	18	19	20
21	22	23	24	25	26	27
28	29	30	31			

Dear Papa God, no matter what trials come my way,
please help me remember that every weakness
requires me to depend on You even more. Amen.

28—SUNDAY

29—MONDAY

30—TUESDAY

31—WEDNESDAY

....
....
....
....

1—THURSDAY

....
....
....
....

2—FRIDAY

....
....
....
....

3—SATURDAY

....
....
....
....

The LORD is good, a refuge in times of trouble.
He cares for those who trust in him.
NAHUM 1:7 NIV

AUGUST 2019

SUNDAY	MONDAY	TUESDAY	WEDNESDAY
28	29	30	31
4	5	6	7
11	12	13	14
18	19	20	21
25	26	27	28

THURSDAY	FRIDAY	SATURDAY
1	2	3
8	9	10
15	16	17
22	23	24
29	30	31

JULY

S	M	T	W	T	F	S
		1	2	3	4	5	6
7	8	9	10	11	12	13
14	15	16	17	18	19	20
21	22	23	24	25	26	27
28	29	30	31

SEPTEMBER

S	M	T	W	T	F	S
1	2	3	4	5	6	7
8	9	10	11	12	13	14
15	16	17	18	19	20	21
22	23	24	25	26	27	28
29	30

TRUST IN GOD'S SOVEREIGNTY

Peace, in the midst of life's chaos. Peace, that jumping-off platform for inexplicable joy. Peace that elusive, anxiety-free place of freedom we long for.

I've been thinking a lot about peace lately. Why is it so hard to grasp? And when we finally do, why does it slip-side away so quickly?

I've learned that real, honest-to-goodness peace is entirely dependent on our trust in God's sovereignty. That means believing He's in control of all the details of our lives, even if it doesn't feel like it. Only when our trust is anchored in Him can we find peace. There's nothing random or accidental about it. Trust is a decision we make. A volitional, intentional act.

GOALS *for this* MONTH

○ ....

○ ....

○ ....

○ ....

○ ....

○ ....

○ ....

○ ....

○ ....

○ ....

○ ....

○ ....

○ ....

○ ....

○ ....

○ ....

*We know that God is always at work for
the good of everyone who loves him.*
ROMANS 8:28 CEV

AUGUST

2019

S	M	T	W	T	F	S
				1	2	3
4	5	6	7	8	9	10
11	12	13	14	15	16	17
18	19	20	21	22	23	24
25	26	27	28	29	30	31

Dear Papa God, no matter what trials come my way,
please help me remember that every weakness
requires me to depend on You even more. Amen.

4—SUNDAY

5—MONDAY

6—TUESDAY

7—WEDNESDAY

8—THURSDAY

9—FRIDAY

10—SATURDAY

Three times I begged the Lord to make this suffering go away. But he replied, "My kindness is all you need. My power is stronger when you are weak."

2 CORINTHIANS 12:8-9 CEV

AUGUST

2019

S	M	T	W	T	F	S
				1	2	3
4	5	6	7	8	9	10
11	12	13	14	15	16	17
18	19	20	21	22	23	24
25	26	27	28	29	30	31

Dear Papa God, I need to hear Your voice loudly
and clearly in this fallen world. Please help me to listen
to and learn from Your Spirit and Your Word. Amen.

11—SUNDAY

....

....

....

....

12—MONDAY

....

....

....

....

13—TUESDAY

....

....

....

....

14—WEDNESDAY

15—THURSDAY

16—FRIDAY

17—SATURDAY

*If you need wisdom, ask our generous God, and he will
give it to you. He will not rebuke you for asking. But when
you ask him, be sure that your faith is in God alone.*

JAMES 1:5-6 NLT

AUGUST

2019

S	M	T	W	T	F	S
				1	2	3
4	5	6	7	8	9	10
11	12	13	14	15	16	17
18	19	20	21	22	23	24
25	26	27	28	29	30	31

Forgiveness is the slipcover for the soul.
We're not defined by our mistakes;
we're recovered and remodeled by forgiveness.

18—SUNDAY

19—MONDAY

20—TUESDAY

21—WEDNESDAY

....
....
....
....

22—THURSDAY

....
....
....
....

23—FRIDAY

....
....
....
....

24—SATURDAY

....
....
....
....

If we confess our sins, He is faithful and righteous to forgive
us our sins and to cleanse us from all unrighteousness.

1 JOHN 1:9 NASB

AUGUST

2019

S	M	T	W	T	F	S
				1	2	3
4	5	6	7	8	9	10
11	12	13	14	15	16	17
18	19	20	21	22	23	24
25	26	27	28	29	30	31

Dear Papa God, when I struggle with worry,
please remind me how big You are and how
Your will prevails in every situation. Amen.

25—SUNDAY

....
....
....
....

26—MONDAY

....
....
....
....

27—TUESDAY

....
....
....
....

28—WEDNESDAY

....

....

....

....

29—THURSDAY

....

....

....

....

30—FRIDAY

....

....

....

....

31—SATURDAY

....

....

....

....

*"Can all your worries add a single moment to your life?
And if worry can't accomplish a little thing like that,
what's the use of worrying over bigger things?"*

LUKE 12:25-26 NLT

SEPTEMBER 2019

SUNDAY	MONDAY	TUESDAY	WEDNESDAY
1	2	3	4
	Labor Day		
8	9	10	11
15	16	17	18
22	23	24	25
	First Day of Autumn		
29	30	1	2

THURSDAY	FRIDAY	SATURDAY
5	6	7
12	13	14
19	20	21
26	27	28
3	4	5

AUGUST

S	M	T	W	T	F	S
					1	2	3
4	5	6	7	8	9	10
11	12	13	14	15	16	17
18	19	20	21	22	23	24
25	26	27	28	29	30	31

OCTOBER

S	M	T	W	T	F	S
		1	2	3	4	5
6	7	8	9	10	11	12
13	14	15	16	17	18	19
20	21	22	23	24	25	26
27	28	29	30	31		

JUST LIKE HANNAH

Hannah not only had to share her husband with another woman, but she was barren—a public disgrace in her day. For many years, she endured the taunting of "the other woman," which caused her constant tears and, no doubt, depression. But she kept on praying until God mercifully blessed her with her heart's desire, a baby boy. Hannah's child grew up to become the mighty prophet Samuel (see Samuel 1).

GOALS *for this* MONTH

- ○ ....
- ○ ....
- ○ ....
- ○ ....
- ○ ....
- ○ ....
- ○ ....
- ○ ....
- ○ ....
- ○ ....
- ○ ....
- ○ ....
- ○ ....
- ○ ....
- ○ ....
- ○ ....
- ○ ....
- ○ ....

*Hannah prayed silently to
the Lord for a long time.*
1 Samuel 1:12 cev

SEPTEMBER

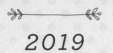

2019

S	M	T	W	T	F	S
1	2	3	4	5	6	7
8	9	10	11	12	13	14
15	16	17	18	19	20	21
22	23	24	25	26	27	28
29	30					

And love—for ourselves as well as
our Creator—is a strong motivator
to help us conquer our fears.

1—SUNDAY

....
....
....
....

2—MONDAY   *Labor Day*

....
....
....
....

3—TUESDAY

....
....
....
....

4—WEDNESDAY

....

....

....

....

5—THURSDAY

....

....

....

....

6—FRIDAY

....

....

....

....

7—SATURDAY

....

....

....

....

Perfect love drives out fear.

1 JOHN 4:18 NIV

SEPTEMBER

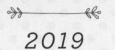

2019

S	M	T	W	T	F	S
1	2	3	4	5	6	7
8	9	10	11	12	13	14
15	16	17	18	19	20	21
22	23	24	25	26	27	28
29	30					

I don't believe Papa God meant for us to thank
only Him for the blessings that enrich our lives,
but also to thank the people responsible for the little
things that make our earth sojourn more pleasant.

8—SUNDAY

9—MONDAY

10—TUESDAY

11—WEDNESDAY

12—THURSDAY

13—FRIDAY

14—SATURDAY

Come, let us sing to the LORD! Let us shout joyfully
to the Rock of our salvation. Let us come to him with
thanksgiving. Let us sing psalms of praise to him.
PSALM 95:1–2 NLT

SEPTEMBER

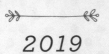

2019

S	M	T	W	T	F	S
1	2	3	4	5	6	7
8	9	10	11	12	13	14
15	16	17	18	19	20	21
22	23	24	25	26	27	28
29	30					

Dear Papa God, there is such power
and peace in counting my blessings.
Thank You for all of them. Amen.

15—SUNDAY

....

....

....

....

16—MONDAY

....

....

....

....

17—TUESDAY

....

....

....

....

18—WEDNESDAY

....

....

....

....

19—THURSDAY

....

....

....

....

20—FRIDAY

....

....

....

....

21—SATURDAY

....

....

....

....

*Give thanks for everything to God the
Father in the name of our Lord Jesus Christ.*

EPHESIANS 5:20 NLT

SEPTEMBER

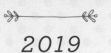

2019

S	M	T	W	T	F	S
1	2	3	4	5	6	7
8	9	10	11	12	13	14
15	16	17	18	19	20	21
22	23	24	25	26	27	28
29	30					

Dear Papa God, please protect me and keep me strong in the fight against the enemy. I can withstand the attacks using the armor only You can give. Amen.

22—SUNDAY

....

....

....

....

23—MONDAY   *First Day of Autumn*

....

....

....

....

24—TUESDAY

....

....

....

....

25—WEDNESDAY

26—THURSDAY

27—FRIDAY

28—SATURDAY

We are not fighting against humans. We are fighting against forces and authorities and against rulers of darkness and powers in the spiritual world.

EPHESIANS 6:12 CEV

OCTOBER 2019

SUNDAY	MONDAY	TUESDAY	WEDNESDAY
29	30	1	2
6	7	8	9
13	14	15	16
	Columbus Day		
20	21	22	23
27	28	29	30

THURSDAY	FRIDAY	SATURDAY
3	4	5
10	11	12
17	18	19
24	25	26
31 *Halloween*	1	2

SEPTEMBER

S	M	T	W	T	F	S
1	2	3	4	5	6	7
8	9	10	11	12	13	14
15	16	17	18	19	20	21
22	23	24	25	26	27	28
29	30					

NOVEMBER

S	M	T	W	T	F	S
					1	2
3	4	5	6	7	8	9
10	11	12	13	14	15	16
17	18	19	20	21	22	23
24	25	26	27	28	29	30

IN BODY AND SPIRIT

Jesus is not just our Messiah, Prince of Peace, and Savior; He's our role model as a human being facing real, heart-slamming adversity, our "God in a bod."

Right after Jesus assured His followers that, although His death was imminent, He wouldn't desert them but would always be with them through the comfort and guidance of the Holy Spirit, He gave the best parting gift ever: "I am leaving you with a gift—peace of mind and heart. And the peace I give is a gift the world cannot give. So don't be troubled or afraid" (John 14:27 NLT).

GOALS *for this* MONTH

○ ....
○ ....
○ ....
○ ....
○ ....
○ ....
○ ....
○ ....
○ ....
○ ....
○ ....
○ ....
○ ....
○ ....
○ ....
○ ....
○ ....

The Lord has promised that
he will not leave us or desert us.
HEBREWS 13:5 CEV

SEPTEMBER–
OCTOBER

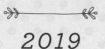

2019

S	M	T	W	T	F	S
		1	2	3	4	5
6	7	8	9	10	11	12
13	14	15	16	17	18	19
20	21	22	23	24	25	26
27	28	29	30	31		

Dear Papa God, sometimes it seems like forgiveness requires a constant battle between my feelings and my actions. Help me to act in obedience and trust You. Amen.

29—SUNDAY

....

....

....

....

30—MONDAY

....

....

....

....

1—TUESDAY

....

....

....

....

2—WEDNESDAY

....
....
....
....

3—THURSDAY

....
....
....
....

4—FRIDAY

....
....
....
....

5—SATURDAY

....
....
....
....

*"If you have anything against someone,
forgive—only then will your heavenly Father be
inclined to also wipe your slate clean of sins."*

MARK 11:25 MSG

OCTOBER

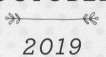

2019

S	M	T	W	T	F	S
		1	2	3	4	5
6	7	8	9	10	11	12
13	14	15	16	17	18	19
20	21	22	23	24	25	26
27	28	29	30	31		

Dear Papa God, please help me to resolve and
let go of this resentment I'm holding. I don't want
it to destroy my relationships with others and
especially my relationship with You. Amen.

6—SUNDAY

....
....
....
....

7—MONDAY

....
....
....
....

8—TUESDAY

....
....
....
....

9—WEDNESDAY

....

....

....

....

10—THURSDAY

....

....

....

....

11—FRIDAY

....

....

....

....

12—SATURDAY

....

....

....

....

*Be patient and trust the Lord. Don't let it bother
you when all goes well for those who do sinful things.
Don't be angry or furious. Anger can lead to sin.*

PSALM 37:7-8 CEV

OCTOBER

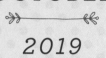

2019

S	M	T	W	T	F	S
		1	2	3	4	5
6	7	8	9	10	11	12
13	14	15	16	17	18	19
20	21	22	23	24	25	26
27	28	29	30	31		

God's Word is our sword—
our biggest and best weapon.

13—SUNDAY

....
....
....
....

14—MONDAY   *Columbus Day*

....
....
....
....

15—TUESDAY

....
....
....
....

16—WEDNESDAY

....
....
....
....

17—THURSDAY

....
....
....
....

18—FRIDAY

....
....
....
....

19—SATURDAY

....
....
....
....

For the word of God is alive and active.
Sharper than any double-edged sword, it penetrates
even to dividing soul and spirit, joints and marrow;
it judges the thoughts and attitudes of the heart.

HEBREWS 4:12 NIV

OCTOBER

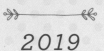

2019

S	M	T	W	T	F	S
		1	2	3	4	5
6	7	8	9	10	11	12
13	14	15	16	17	18	19
20	21	22	23	24	25	26
27	28	29	30	31		

Dear Papa God, every blessing I have ultimately comes from You. Please give me wisdom about my finances and open hands to give generously of what You've trusted to my care. Amen.

20—SUNDAY

....

....

....

....

21—MONDAY

....

....

....

....

22—TUESDAY

....

....

....

....

23—WEDNESDAY

....
....
....
....

24—THURSDAY

....
....
....
....

25—FRIDAY

....
....
....
....

26—SATURDAY

....
....
....
....

"I came naked from my mother's womb, and I will be naked when I leave. The LORD gave me what I had, and the LORD has taken it away. Praise the name of the LORD!"

JOB 1:21 NLT

OCTOBER–NOVEMBER

2019

S	M	T	W	T	F	S
		1	2	3	4	5
6	7	8	9	10	11	12
13	14	15	16	17	18	19
20	21	22	23	24	25	26
27	28	29	30	31		

You can't control what God does or doesn't do.
Because He is God. He's the One in control.
He always has been and always will be.

27—SUNDAY

....
....
....
....

28—MONDAY

....
....
....
....

29—TUESDAY

....
....
....
....

30—WEDNESDAY

....
....
....
....

31—THURSDAY   *Halloween*

....
....
....
....

1—FRIDAY

....
....
....
....

2—SATURDAY

....
....
....
....

My God will meet all your needs according
to the riches of his glory in Christ Jesus.
PHILIPPIANS 4:19 NIV

NOVEMBER 2019

SUNDAY	MONDAY	TUESDAY	WEDNESDAY
27	28	29	30
3	4	5 *Election Day*	6
10	11 *Veterans Day*	12	13
17	18	19	20
24	25	26	27

THURSDAY	FRIDAY	SATURDAY
31	1	2
7	8	9
14	15	16
21	22	23
28	29	30
Thanksgiving Day		

OCTOBER

S	M	T	W	T	F	S
		1	2	3	4	5
6	7	8	9	10	11	12
13	14	15	16	17	18	19
20	21	22	23	24	25	26
27	28	29	30	31		

DECEMBER

S	M	T	W	T	F	S
1	2	3	4	5	6	7
8	9	10	11	12	13	14
15	16	17	18	19	20	21
22	23	24	25	26	27	28
29	30	31				

HE WILL FIND YOU

Like the parable Jesus told about the lost sheep (meaning us!) in the fifteenth chapter of Luke (read verses 1–6 to refresh your memory), we can never stray away from our Shepherd to the point of no return. He loves us far too much to let us go. I find that marvelously reassuring, don't you?

So when you lose your way and begin to wander, whether it's spiritually, emotionally, mentally, or physically (hey, I can get lost in a tote bag), be assured that Papa will find you. Know why? Because you, sister, are too loved to be lost.

GOALS *for this* MONTH

- ○ ....
- ○ ....
- ○ ....
- ○ ....
- ○ ....
- ○ ....
- ○ ....
- ○ ....
- ○ ....
- ○ ....
- ○ ....
- ○ ....
- ○ ....
- ○ ....
- ○ ....
- ○ ....
- ○ ....

*Our LORD, we belong to you. We tell you
what worries us, and you won't let us fall.*

PSALM 55:22 CEV

NOVEMBER

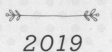

2019

S	M	T	W	T	F	S
					1	2
3	4	5	6	7	8	9
10	11	12	13	14	15	16
17	18	19	20	21	22	23
24	25	26	27	28	29	30

Dear Papa God, I want to live confidently,
not fearfully, because of the Spirit of power, love, and
self-discipline You have given me. Thank You. Amen.

3—SUNDAY

....

....

....

....

4—MONDAY

....

....

....

....

5—TUESDAY   *Election Day*

....

....

....

....

6—WEDNESDAY

7—THURSDAY

8—FRIDAY

9—SATURDAY

For God has not given us a spirit of fear and timidity,
but of power, love, and self-discipline.

2 TIMOTHY 1:7 NLT

NOVEMBER

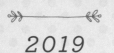

2019

S	M	T	W	T	F	S
					1	2
3	4	5	6	7	8	9
10	11	12	13	14	15	16
17	18	19	20	21	22	23
24	25	26	27	28	29	30

The gifts the Lord specifically gives each of us are rarely on the surface. He has lovingly nestled virtues like discernment, kindness, or graciousness within our character.

10—SUNDAY

....

....

....

....

11—MONDAY   *Veterans Day*

....

....

....

....

12—TUESDAY

....

....

....

....

13—WEDNESDAY

14—THURSDAY

15—FRIDAY

16—SATURDAY

"The Lord does not look at the things people look at.
People look at the outward appearance,
but the Lord looks at the heart."

1 SAMUEL 16:7 NIV

NOVEMBER

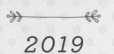

2019

S	M	T	W	T	F	S
					1	2
3	4	5	6	7	8	9
10	11	12	13	14	15	16
17	18	19	20	21	22	23
24	25	26	27	28	29	30

Dear Papa God, I want You and You alone to receive my worship. Please draw me back to You when I stray toward focusing too much on myself and my appearance. Amen.

17—SUNDAY

....
....
....
....

18—MONDAY

....
....
....
....

19—TUESDAY

....
....
....
....

20—WEDNESDAY

....

....

....

....

21—THURSDAY

....

....

....

....

22—FRIDAY

....

....

....

....

23—SATURDAY

....

....

....

....

Charm is deceptive, and beauty is fleeting;
but a woman who fears the LORD is to be praised.
PROVERBS 31:30 NIV

NOVEMBER

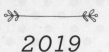

2019

S	M	T	W	T	F	S
					1	2
3	4	5	6	7	8	9
10	11	12	13	14	15	16
17	18	19	20	21	22	23
24	25	26	27	28	29	30

God doesn't believe in labels. When we invite Jesus
into our hearts and ask Him to fill us with His love,
all God sees when He looks at us is the gentle,
sweet, beautiful reflection of His Son.

24—SUNDAY

25—MONDAY

26—TUESDAY

27—WEDNESDAY

....

....

....

....

28—THURSDAY   *Thanksgiving Day*

....

....

....

....

29—FRIDAY

....

....

....

....

30—SATURDAY

....

....

....

....

For God made Christ, who never sinned,
to be the offering for our sin, so that we
could be made right with God through Christ.

2 CORINTHIANS 5:21 NLT

DECEMBER 2019

SUNDAY	MONDAY	TUESDAY	WEDNESDAY
1	2	3	4
8	9	10	11
15	16	17	18
22 *Hanukkah Begins at Sundown*	23	24 *Christmas Eve*	25 *Christmas Day*
29	30	31 *New Year's Eve*	1

THURSDAY	FRIDAY	SATURDAY
5	6	7
12	13	14
19	20	21 *First Day of Winter*
26	27	28
2	3	4

NOVEMBER

S	M	T	W	T	F	S
					1	2
3	4	5	6	7	8	9
10	11	12	13	14	15	16
17	18	19	20	21	22	23
24	25	26	27	28	29	30

JANUARY

S	M	T	W	T	F	S
			1	2	3	4
5	6	7	8	9	10	11
12	13	14	15	16	17	18
19	20	21	22	23	24	25
26	27	28	29	30	31	

ANSWERED PRAYER

I know that sometimes we don't feel thankful for God's answers, especially when troubles fill us with fear, anger, or resentment. But Papa God didn't specify that we should be thankful only for the good answers. No, He said to thank Him for all His answers, even when it's *"No, My beloved child," "Wait on My perfect timing,"* or *"I'm sorry you must go through this fire, precious one, but I will go through it with you."* We don't have to feel happy about tough circumstances, but if we view the fire-treading moments when we're thankful-by-will-only as acts of faith, believing that our all-powerful, all-knowing Papa God is using even the grinding process of the tough times to sharpen our trust, we will draw closer to Him. And hey, isn't that our goal?

GOALS *for this* MONTH

- ○ ....
- ○ ....
- ○ ....
- ○ ....
- ○ ....
- ○ ....
- ○ ....
- ○ ....
- ○ ....
- ○ ....
- ○ ....
- ○ ....
- ○ ....
- ○ ....
- ○ ....
- ○ ....
- ○ ....
- ○ ....

Tell God what you need,
and thank him for all he has done.

PHILIPPIANS 4:6 NLT

DECEMBER

2019

S	M	T	W	T	F	S
1	2	3	4	5	6	7
8	9	10	11	12	13	14
15	16	17	18	19	20	21
22	23	24	25	26	27	28
29	30	31				

When you ask Jesus to fill you with His presence,
you have a new identity: a pure, healthy, holy,
confident identity. The old labels are obsolete.

1—SUNDAY

....
....
....
....

2—MONDAY

....
....
....
....

3—TUESDAY

....
....
....
....

4—WEDNESDAY

....

....

....

....

5—THURSDAY

....

....

....

....

6—FRIDAY

....

....

....

....

7—SATURDAY

....

....

....

....

Anyone who belongs to Christ is a new person.
The past is forgotten, and everything is new.
2 CORINTHIANS 5:17 CEV

DECEMBER

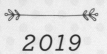

2019

S	M	T	W	T	F	S
1	2	3	4	5	6	7
8	9	10	11	12	13	14
15	16	17	18	19	20	21
22	23	24	25	26	27	28
29	30	31				

Real beauty comes only from God's inside-out love.

8—SUNDAY

....
....
....
....

9—MONDAY

....
....
....
....

10—TUESDAY

....
....
....
....

11—WEDNESDAY

....
....
....
....

12—THURSDAY

....
....
....
....

13—FRIDAY

....
....
....
....

14—SATURDAY

....
....
....
....

*Though outwardly we are wasting away,
yet inwardly we are being renewed day by day.*

2 CORINTHIANS 4:16 NIV

DECEMBER

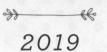

2019

S	M	T	W	T	F	S
1	2	3	4	5	6	7
8	9	10	11	12	13	14
15	16	17	18	19	20	21
22	23	24	25	26	27	28
29	30	31				

Dear Papa God, it's a daily struggle not to do things for my own glory. Please help my attitudes and actions to bring praise to You and You alone. Amen.

15—SUNDAY

....
....
....
....

16—MONDAY

....
....
....
....

17—TUESDAY

....
....
....
....

18—WEDNESDAY

19—THURSDAY

20—FRIDAY

21—SATURDAY   *First Day of Winter*

We take captive every thought to
make it obedient to Christ.
2 CORINTHIANS 10:5 NIV

DECEMBER

2019

S	M	T	W	T	F	S
1	2	3	4	5	6	7
8	9	10	11	12	13	14
15	16	17	18	19	20	21
22	23	24	25	26	27	28
29	30	31				

Dear Papa God, temptation is a strong force, but Your
Word is stronger. Please help me to avoid temptation,
and when I do experience it, please help me to
be ready to fight it and beat it! Amen.

22—SUNDAY   *Hanukkah Begins at Sundown*

....

....

....

....

23—MONDAY

....

....

....

....

24—TUESDAY   *Christmas Eve*

....

....

....

....

25—WEDNESDAY   *Christmas Day*

....

....

....

....

26—THURSDAY

....

....

....

....

27—FRIDAY

....

....

....

....

28—SATURDAY

....

....

....

....

"Watch and pray so that you will not fall into temptation.
The spirit is willing, but the flesh is weak."
MATTHEW 26:41 NIV

JANUARY 2020

SUNDAY	MONDAY	TUESDAY	WEDNESDAY
29	30	31	1 *New Year's Day*
5	6	7	8
12	13	14	15
19	20 *Martin Luther King Jr. Day*	21	22
26	27	28	29

THURSDAY	FRIDAY	SATURDAY
2	3	4
9	10	11
16	17	18
23	24	25
30	31	1

DECEMBER

S	M	T	W	T	F	S
1	2	3	4	5	6	7
8	9	10	11	12	13	14
15	16	17	18	19	20	21
22	23	24	25	26	27	28
29	30	31				

FEBRUARY

S	M	T	W	T	F	S
						1
2	3	4	5	6	7	8
9	10	11	12	13	14	15
16	17	18	19	20	21	22
23	24	25	26	27	28	29

KEEP YOUR HELMET ON

"I think it all boils down to: Who are we going to trust?" Marianna shared with me in her soft voice. "God knows exactly what we think and feel. Peace comes in accepting the path He's set out for us and realizing that none of it was done to hurt us or make us miserable. We have to trust that He'll fill in the holes."

You know, it's no coincidence that the piece of spiritual armor representing salvation through grace is a helmet. We need sturdy, impenetrable headgear to protect our thoughts, reasoning, and motives from the destructive fear of potential disaster. That thick brain padding in our helmet is the assurance that through life, death, or near misses, we're safe in Papa God's hands.

GOALS *for this* MONTH

○ ....

○ ....

○ ....

○ ....

○ ....

○ ....

○ ....

○ ....

○ ....

○ ....

○ ....

○ ....

○ ....

○ ....

○ ....

○ ....

○ ....

○ ....

Take the helmet of salvation and the sword
of the Spirit, which is the word of God.
EPHESIANS 6:17 NIV

DECEMBER 2019–JANUARY

2020

S	M	T	W	T	F	S
			1	2	3	4
5	6	7	8	9	10	11
12	13	14	15	16	17	18
19	20	21	22	23	24	25
26	27	28	29	30	31	

Dear Papa God, there is never a time or reason I should not be praying. Help me to realize that I can and should be in constant conversation with You. Amen.

29—SUNDAY

30—MONDAY

31—TUESDAY   *New Year's Eve*

1—WEDNESDAY

New Year's Day

....

....

....

....

2—THURSDAY

....

....

....

....

3—FRIDAY

....

....

....

....

4—SATURDAY

....

....

....

....

*Let your hope make you glad. Be patient
in time of trouble and never stop praying.*

ROMANS 12:12 CEV

JANUARY

2020

S	M	T	W	T	F	S
			1	2	3	4
5	6	7	8	9	10	11
12	13	14	15	16	17	18
19	20	21	22	23	24	25
26	27	28	29	30	31	

Dear Papa God, please help me to keep the helmet of salvation always covering my head and thus my thoughts, giving me constant confidence that I am saved by You and safe in Your care. Amen.

5—SUNDAY

....

....

....

....

6—MONDAY

....

....

....

....

7—TUESDAY

....

....

....

....

8—WEDNESDAY

....

....

....

....

9—THURSDAY

....

....

....

....

10—FRIDAY

....

....

....

....

11—SATURDAY

....

....

....

....

Cast your cares on the Lord and he will sustain you;
he will never let the righteous be shaken.

PSALM 55:22 NIV

JANUARY

2020

S	M	T	W	T	F	S
			1	2	3	4
5	6	7	8	9	10	11
12	13	14	15	16	17	18
19	20	21	22	23	24	25
26	27	28	29	30	31	

When we sincerely ask the Holy
Spirit to fill us with the joy of the Lord,
and commit to focus on that joy, He'll do it.

12—SUNDAY

13—MONDAY

14—TUESDAY

15—WEDNESDAY

....
....
....
....

16—THURSDAY

....
....
....
....

17—FRIDAY

....
....
....
....

18—SATURDAY

....
....
....
....

You make known to me the path of life;
you will fill me with joy in your presence,
with eternal pleasures at your right hand.

PSALM 16:11 NIV

JANUARY

2020

S	M	T	W	T	F	S
			1	2	3	4
5	6	7	8	9	10	11
12	13	14	15	16	17	18
19	20	21	22	23	24	25
26	27	28	29	30	31	

Dear Papa God, a mother sure needs extra doses of
patience to be able to teach her kids through all
sorts of mistakes and behavior issues while loving
them in generous and wise ways. Please help! Amen.

19—SUNDAY

20—MONDAY   *Martin Luther King Jr. Day*

21—TUESDAY

22—WEDNESDAY

....
....
....
....

23—THURSDAY

....
....
....
....

24—FRIDAY

....
....
....
....

25—SATURDAY

....
....
....
....

*Patience and gentle talk can convince
a ruler and overcome any problem.*

PROVERBS 25:15 CEV

JANUARY– FEBRUARY

2020

S	M	T	W	T	F	S
			1	2	3	4
5	6	7	8	9	10	11
12	13	14	15	16	17	18
19	20	21	22	23	24	25
26	27	28	29	30	31	

Dear Papa God, please forgive me when I lash out in impatience. Help me to grow in courageous patience, trusting that Your timing is always best. Amen.

26—SUNDAY

....
....
....
....

27—MONDAY

....
....
....
....

28—TUESDAY

....
....
....
....

29—WEDNESDAY

....
....
....
....

30—THURSDAY

....
....
....
....

31—FRIDAY

....
....
....
....

1—SATURDAY

....
....
....
....

*Let your hope make you glad. Be patient in
time of trouble and never stop praying.*
ROMANS 12:12 CEV

CONTACTS

Name:

Address:

Phone: Cell:

Email:

Name:

Address:

Phone: Cell:

Email:

Name:

Address:

Phone: Cell:

Email:

Name:

Address:

Phone: Cell:

Email:

CONTACTS

Name:

Address:

Phone: Cell:

Email:

Name:

Address:

Phone: Cell:

Email:

Name:

Address:

Phone: Cell:

Email:

Name:

Address:

Phone: Cell:

Email:

CONTACTS

Name:

Address:

Phone: Cell:

Email:

Name:

Address:

Phone: Cell:

Email:

Name:

Address:

Phone: Cell:

Email:

Name:

Address:

Phone: Cell:

Email:

CONTACTS

Name:

Address:

Phone: Cell:

Email:

Name:

Address:

Phone: Cell:

Email:

Name:

Address:

Phone: Cell:

Email:

Name:

Address:

Phone: Cell:

Email:

CONTACTS

Name:

Address:

Phone: Cell:

Email:

Name:

Address:

Phone: Cell:

Email:

Name:

Address:

Phone: Cell:

Email:

Name:

Address:

Phone: Cell:

Email:

CONTACTS

Name:

Address:

Phone: Cell:

Email:

Name:

Address:

Phone: Cell:

Email:

Name:

Address:

Phone: Cell:

Email:

Name:

Address:

Phone: Cell:

Email:

CONTACTS

Name:

Address:

Phone: Cell:

Email:

Name:

Address:

Phone: Cell:

Email:

Name:

Address:

Phone: Cell:

Email:

Name:

Address:

Phone: Cell:

Email:

CONTACTS

Name:

Address:

Phone: Cell:

Email:

Name:

Address:

Phone: Cell:

Email:

Name:

Address:

Phone: Cell:

Email:

Name:

Address:

Phone: Cell:

Email:

CONTACTS

Name:

Address:

Phone: Cell:

Email:

Name:

Address:

Phone: Cell:

Email:

Name:

Address:

Phone: Cell:

Email:

Name:

Address:

Phone: Cell:

Email:

CONTACTS

Name:

Address:

Phone: Cell:

Email:

Name:

Address:

Phone: Cell:

Email:

Name:

Address:

Phone: Cell:

Email:

Name:

Address:

Phone: Cell:

Email:

2020

JANUARY						
S	M	T	W	T	F	S
			1	2	3	4
5	6	7	8	9	10	11
12	13	14	15	16	17	18
19	20	21	22	23	24	25
26	27	28	29	30	31	

FEBRUARY						
S	M	T	W	T	F	S
						1
2	3	4	5	6	7	8
9	10	11	12	13	14	15
16	17	18	19	20	21	22
23	24	25	26	27	28	29

MARCH						
S	M	T	W	T	F	S
1	2	3	4	5	6	7
8	9	10	11	12	13	14
15	16	17	18	19	20	21
22	23	24	25	26	27	28
29	30	31				

APRIL						
S	M	T	W	T	F	S
			1	2	3	4
5	6	7	8	9	10	11
12	13	14	15	16	17	18
19	20	21	22	23	24	25
26	27	28	29	30		

MAY						
S	M	T	W	T	F	S
					1	2
3	4	5	6	7	8	9
10	11	12	13	14	15	16
17	18	19	20	21	22	23
24	25	26	27	28	29	30
31						

JUNE						
S	M	T	W	T	F	S
	1	2	3	4	5	6
7	8	9	10	11	12	13
14	15	16	17	18	19	20
21	22	23	24	25	26	27
28	29	30				

JULY						
S	M	T	W	T	F	S
			1	2	3	4
5	6	7	8	9	10	11
12	13	14	15	16	17	18
19	20	21	22	23	24	25
26	27	28	29	30	31	

AUGUST						
S	M	T	W	T	F	S
						1
2	3	4	5	6	7	8
9	10	11	12	13	14	15
16	17	18	19	20	21	22
23	24	25	26	27	28	29
30	31					

SEPTEMBER						
S	M	T	W	T	F	S
		1	2	3	4	5
6	7	8	9	10	11	12
13	14	15	16	17	18	19
20	21	22	23	24	25	26
27	28	29	30			

OCTOBER						
S	M	T	W	T	F	S
				1	2	3
4	5	6	7	8	9	10
11	12	13	14	15	16	17
18	19	20	21	22	23	24
25	26	27	28	29	30	31

NOVEMBER						
S	M	T	W	T	F	S
1	2	3	4	5	6	7
8	9	10	11	12	13	14
15	16	17	18	19	20	21
22	23	24	25	26	27	28
29	30					

DECEMBER						
S	M	T	W	T	F	S
		1	2	3	4	5
6	7	8	9	10	11	12
13	14	15	16	17	18	19
20	21	22	23	24	25	26
27	28	29	30	31		

2021

JANUARY						
S	M	T	W	T	F	S
					1	2
3	4	5	6	7	8	9
10	11	12	13	14	15	16
17	18	19	20	21	22	23
24	25	26	27	28	29	30
31						

FEBRUARY						
S	M	T	W	T	F	S
	1	2	3	4	5	6
7	8	9	10	11	12	13
14	15	16	17	18	19	20
21	22	23	24	25	26	27
28						

MARCH						
S	M	T	W	T	F	S
	1	2	3	4	5	6
7	8	9	10	11	12	13
14	15	16	17	18	19	20
21	22	23	24	25	26	27
28	29	30	31			

APRIL						
S	M	T	W	T	F	S
				1	2	3
4	5	6	7	8	9	10
11	12	13	14	15	16	17
18	19	20	21	22	23	24
25	26	27	28	29	30	

MAY						
S	M	T	W	T	F	S
						1
2	3	4	5	6	7	8
9	10	11	12	13	14	15
16	17	18	19	20	21	22
23	24	25	26	27	28	29
30	31					

JUNE						
S	M	T	W	T	F	S
		1	2	3	4	5
6	7	8	9	10	11	12
13	14	15	16	17	18	19
20	21	22	23	24	25	26
27	28	29	30			

JULY						
S	M	T	W	T	F	S
				1	2	3
4	5	6	7	8	9	10
11	12	13	14	15	16	17
18	19	20	21	22	23	24
25	26	27	28	29	30	31

AUGUST						
S	M	T	W	T	F	S
1	2	3	4	5	6	7
8	9	10	11	12	13	14
15	16	17	18	19	20	21
22	23	24	25	26	27	28
29	30	31				

SEPTEMBER						
S	M	T	W	T	F	S
			1	2	3	4
5	6	7	8	9	10	11
12	13	14	15	16	17	18
19	20	21	22	23	24	25
26	27	28	29	30		

OCTOBER						
S	M	T	W	T	F	S
					1	2
3	4	5	6	7	8	9
10	11	12	13	14	15	16
17	18	19	20	21	22	23
24	25	26	27	28	29	30
31						

NOVEMBER						
S	M	T	W	T	F	S
	1	2	3	4	5	6
7	8	9	10	11	12	13
14	15	16	17	18	19	20
21	22	23	24	25	26	27
28	29	30				

DECEMBER						
S	M	T	W	T	F	S
			1	2	3	4
5	6	7	8	9	10	11
12	13	14	15	16	17	18
19	20	21	22	23	24	25
26	27	28	29	30	31